What Palms Know

What Palms Know

Paul Boor

ISBN: 978-1-962148-25-2
LOC: 2026940183

Editor:Britton Larson
Cover Designer: Kelso Mayo

Lamar University Literary Press
Beaumont, TX

Thanks to the late Rita Daly, my first English teacher, for wanting to hear me; to Dr. John Gorman and the late Dr. Malcolm Broderick, who started and led the Galveston Poets Roundtable through years of readings, hurricanes, and Mardi Gras. I must also gratefully acknowledge the modern sonneteers, but especially Henri Cole, whose thoughts on the sonnet make it, for me, a powerful canvas, fitted perfectly on the page .... And thanks to my one true love, all of them.

Recent Poetry from Lamar University Literary Press

Lisa Adams, *Xuai*
Walter Bargen, *My Other Mother's Red Mercedes*
Christine Boldt, *In Every Tatter*
Devan Burton, *A Room for Us*
Jerry Bradley, *Collapsing into Possibility*
Mark Busby, *Through Our Times*
Julie Chappell, *Mad Habits of a Life*
Stan Crawford, *Resisting Gravity*
Glover Davis, *Academy of Dreams*
William Virgil Davis, *The Bones Poems*
Chris Ellery, *Elder Tree*
Dede Fox, *On Wings of Silence*
Alan Gann, *That's Entertainment*
Larry Griffin, *Cedar Plums*
Michelle Hartman, *Irony and Irrelevance*
Lynn Hoggard, *First Light*
Michael Jennings, *Crossings: A Record of Travel*
Gretchen Johnson, *A Trip Through Downer, Minnesota*
Markham Johnson, *Dear Dreamland*
Betsy Joseph & Chip Dameron, *Relatively Speaking*
Ulf Kirchdorfer, *Chewing Green Leaves*
Jim McGarrah, *A Balancing Act*
J. Pittman McGehee, *Nod of Knowing*
Laurence Musgrove, *Bluebonnet Sutras*
Benjamin Myers, *The Family Book of Martyrs*
Janice Northerns, *Some Electric Hum*
Godspower Oboido, *Wandering Feet on Pebbled Shores*
Carol Coffee Reposa, *Sailing West*
Jan Seale, *Particulars*
Steven Schroeder, *the moon, not the finger, pointing*
Glen Sorestad, *Hazards of Eden*
Vincent Spina, *The Sumptuous Hills of Gulfport*
W.K. Stratton, *Betrayal Creek*
Wally Swist, *Invocation*
Ken Waldman, *Sports Page*
Loretta Diane Walker, *Ode to My Mother's Voice*
Dan Williams, *At the Gates, a Refuge of Milkweed and Sunflowers*
Jonas Zdanys, *The Angled Road*
For information on these and other Lamar University Literary Press
books go to www.Lamar.edu/literarypress

Acknowledgements

Arrowsmith

Bayousphere

Blue Mountain

blueLINE

Equinox

Exquisite Corpse

Houston Poetry Fest Anthology

i.e. Magazine

Open Forum

Penumbra

Poetry Motel

Rhino

Sol Magazine (electronic)

Sulphur River

The Gopherwood Review

The Journal of Medical Humanities

The Redneck Review of Literature

Thirteen

Tidelines: An Anthology of Galveston Writers

Whole Notes

CONTENTS

I. Hurricane Prone

II. Dreamland

III. The Music

Hurricane Prone

What Palms Know

there's little new
to dream   now it's all
redreamt   in a sort of
generic sleep where:
                nails scrap the down
                from shoulder blades
                & damp palms lie
                along the spine's
                white line

ten years ago
she made her point
on the common ground
of a downtown diner:
                outside
                a clattering
                psalm of palm fronds
                was raised
                in tropical praise
                of a trial separation

dreamless
to sit and type
late at night
last of the ribbon
dryly ticking

Mud Flats

This is the season
of leaves rattling
on clicking pods
of brown grasses
that scrape against
things dry & hopeless.

Autumn
drifts endlessly forward
but we have paused
in a vain attempt
to return to a place
we passed before
(as dogs in the woods
retrace their steps
to exit).

Failure
is an acrid fruit
in our mouths
as we plan a season
of separation.

The heat of summer
brought us change
with no warning
& now the cool sun
of autumn
drives a steady
pungent breeze
over dry and lonely
mud flats.

Hail Storm

all afternoon the screens
black with flies
were humming:
        a storm was coming

into eyes dilated
by sleep lightning
white as death poured
while hailstones
the size of
        butterbeans
        hit
        the air conditioner

half the night we lay
(pillows over heads)
antique window glass
ringing like cymbals
as the squall lines
passed through
        muffled
                like hangovers
                        two days old

after frontal passage
the scummy swamp's
like tropical punch:
        ice balls bob
        on sweet still pools
        where tomorrow
                mosquitoes
                        will bloom

HOT

-1-

Tired from this heat
I mean drained . . .
So damn hot I'm
oscillating
instead of the fan.
Hot. Puking hot.
Out on the sidewalk
you're rudely
        cooked.

-2-

Up the stairs
hotter and hotter
my hand aching
from this glass
of crushed ice:
        gin and bitter lemon
        juniper, and hurry!
        seeds and bark
        peel and powder
        Moroccan fullsome berry

and tell you this:
        licorice.

-3-

Jogged this morning
all afternoon
flat on the couch
fan on full
ball game roaring
my crankcase drained
and the cramps start:
        abominable pain
        of dehydration
        like an iron foot
        standing on my
        solar plexus.

-4-

Hot I mean hot I lie down on the park bench for a siesta in the middle of the afternoon the sun is baking everything but the heavy canopy makes the bench look good: dark as night looking out at the brightness of the afternoon from under the black-trunked oaks and rattling palms. . . Hot I mean hot I fall asleep and dream unpleasantries restless and sweating a dark ring on the collar wetter and wetter and hot hot hot in my sneakers even with no socks so I figure I'll wake up and get these bad dream over with but no way no way there's no waking up . . . Come to find out I died of heat stroke while siesta-ing just melted right there on the bench and dripped over the edge and squeezed down through the slats onto the sidewalk underneath like molten lava. Vulcanized debris is what I am and did you hear that a serious source of air pollution in Japan is the mercury from dental fillings vapourized from the smoke stacks of crematoriums? . . So here I am not vapourized exactly but clearly melted and dripped into blobs (the sum of the parts formed under the bench much smaller than the original whole) agatized flesh balls lie on the grass like the slag that once flew from the stacks of railroad engines across the country: blown from red hot stacks and landing in the woods along the track. Coating nearby plants and small animals I immortalize them in a rock hard slag-ball, like how they encase living creatures, e.g., scorpions, and other true-to-life items like cattle turds forever trapped inside polymerized clear plastic domes for use as paperweights on the desks of the busy executives of Houston.

Suddenly a Rhythm

The ceiling fan beats dead air
                    against clogged screens
beyond, palm fronds droop
like idle wings in the late afternoon
& you're at your desk immobilized by fear
aging fast in your ill-fitting skin   your fool's
itinerary for the day forgotten while you recall
how the world was your oyster
and you couldn't find your oyster knife

Outside   children play deep into your middle age
they are circling the house, their path worn into gray
clay, when you feel your pupils dilating
in the softening light   dilating
with a vision of all the antique children
who have acted like idiots in this backyard

Suddenly   there's a rhythm
it hangs in the air like Salsa de Cuba
a rhythm   suddenly there
a beat to set a foot to tapping
a rhythm   to this living

You know there is no rhyme to it
                    just
                                a rhythm

Rainy Day In A Tourist Town

A rainy day and the town is ours
we think, looking out
from under the dripping palms
                                        at the real thing

In the projects   leaves dance
on empty courts   hamburger wrappers
swirl   over wet macadam

Galleries closed museums empty
the barmaids chew gum slow
We dream of spring break, neck break,
any break in the overcast
then   grey skies blacken blacker
and it's raining down tourists
sunburns aglow, flipflops
tumbling from the sky, they alight
to glide down watery streets
                as if it were their home too

Tropical Stew

Since dawn
the Island City simmers
while morning meats are mixed
    chopped sausage
    (smoky, hot, and mild, too)
    lightly colored hunks of loin
    tendon dense and sinewy
    the tough collagenous knuckle
    with clinging dermal bits

Stirred by our thunderstorm
topped up by a five minute downpour
then . . . toss in the tomatoes
    okra onion spleen-shaped beans
    floating floating floating

Turn up the heat
til it all rolls round
after noon check the meat
wow
our tropical stew pops
splatters sauce
and the smell
    sinew to loin
    tendon to bean
    we're cooking now

It takes all day
and then it has to sit
thickening (sinking shin bone)
til the sauce (ah the sauce
red and fiery)   clears

In the warm and pungent
urban evening's savory
and sweet odoriferous mix
hungry diners stir
their gaily colored
downtown
    now cooler
    but still warm enough
    and tasty oh so tasty

County Fair, the Honey Exhibit

he sat in the full golden light
of his mason jars
his wrinkled queen on her throne
beside him   speaking of bees

a lotta cotton in that honey he said
            and ragweed said his queen

their faces were red soil
cracked by drought
their farm
a flat ungentle land
where crawfish build crumbling towers
toward the Texas sun

in their voices was the dull hum of wings
the beat of a hive of drones
huddled in waxen combs
like single men in rented rooms
each playing out a lottery
where only one is chosen
to roil in the sweetness
           of an immortal lover

Skeleton Crewe

on the weirdest night of the year
THE JUGGLER comes out to ride
he whirls down fog filled streets
on a stolen unicycle, opposable jaws clicking
the painful wind of exercise howling in his joints
he tosses 8 stone balls high: circling, uncountable
they sail over banks and museums
to burst like beads of plastic in the eyes of tourists

Liberace (flash of fingers over greased keys,
teeth blinding) rises from the dead
to join THE JUGGLER and the two lead
the great promenade of the Fat Tuesday Ball

transvestites gather in the great hall
feathers and silk drift over taut falsies
they pose for close-ups, then
the promenade files off the stage & orbits
the saucy taco chips as hot dogs boil
and dips fantasize on the cheese soufflé

King Neptune toys with Mark Antony
(chains over smooth bare breast)
while waitress, chef, owner (even tourists)
await the judgement of the ball

a softly-fattened slug of a judge gargles
through the microphone:
        Liberace wins! (we all knew he would)

throughout the night THE JUGGLER rides:
        sore bones clicking on plates of cartilage
        he fills the cisterns of the city
                with a bilious Lenten champagne

The Bungee Jumper

teeters atop his rented crane
for this one second
he is part of the sky

on the edge of his death wish
he sees the horizon buckle
            the beach tilt
then he pitches
with westward yaw
and is falling spread-eagled
in the open wind
            his fifty dollar decision
                        firm

his arms beat small circles
his red t-shirt bleeds
            into the clouds
at odds with gravity
he falls   and falls
tied by a thread unraveling
at different speeds
for each of us

The Oyster

was a good idea.
Noah took a sack
on board   sparing
only two   for the landing.

Silly sexy oysters
lying in their salty beds
stomachs full and livers fat
gonads about to pop
all night and day
they filter filter filter
their tiny two-chambered
hearts   beating
in unison   the entire reef
          in simultaneous
                    systole.

In the cool fresh water flood
of fall   their hinges yawn
and they flush themselves
of summer's cholerous tides
          & a smelter's burden
          of mercury
                    cadmium
                              lead.

Now! Listen! Low boats are growling
overhead   sharp rakes drag deep
opening the silent beds
and these silly sea cunts
these bivalved nuggets
with dockside value so sweet
clamp down   tensing
          like submariners
          waiting for a depth charge.

John’s Oyster Resort

Platters of opalescent
grey creatures shimmer
in the dim staccato light
of beating ceiling fans.
From their crushed-ice beds
it’s a short slide to digestive juices.

The air, deep-fried, congeals
on the diners’ faces
        the beer’s
        gone flat
        with the heat.

When lifted
the chilled rock animal
shows off its fluted edges:
        sharply carved templates
        of some Goliath’s face
Tipped and ready for the slide
the shell flows over;
rising oyster liquor
shorts out fans and lights
while diners, waitress, cashier
scull about as they drown:

        this is the penalty accrued
        for tender lives & salty serum shed
        by an ancient coastal harvest.

Drifts/Dunes

Pulverized oystershell
fine silty waves of it
sift into your sneakers
your feet are baking
& fat locusts strike
like sparrows
their whirring wings
beating the numb air.

These dunes are ever shifting.
They rise hardpacked on windward
and drop off softly on the lee.
Their ancient grey sand sprouts
sticky burrs and shingles
blown from mexican roofs
by the hurricanes:
        asphalt sails
        riding the gulf stream.

If the wind shifts
the dunes bend backward
the sand erodes
and ripples with ugly gouges:
        grey scalloped edges
        softly packing down.

If the wind dies
mosquitos bloom
and strange air-born webs
unfurl to snag your arms your legs
Tight as nylon fishline
        they drag down tourists
        & choke their motorcycles
        in the bloody hot sand.

Metallic massacre:
        mixed in salt air
        rust and carrion
        are ravenously oxidized
        in the lean white meat
        of land crabs.

Dream Review

Open your eyes, you're in a room
full of strangers.
In your sleep you wrote
the perfect scene (it seemed)
but under further review
things came apart pretty fast
in the frightening light of morning
in a room full of strangers.

Open your eyes and yes the day's gone
you're on your way home
despondent, you take the interstate
at 80, embedded in petrochemical haze
the whole way back to your backwater
town, your fetid bayou
where rawboned birds slump on the dock
their deformed beaks sieving dark water.

It's dusk so grab a beer,
kick back & couch! watch clouds
of insects skim the water.
You can look forward to your new videos
(compelling adult entertainment)
because you've twisted an endless
secret from its source, you've
tested the darkness for its depth.

Open your eyes
        you've written the perfect scene.

You Dreamt of Goalposts

Start somewhere somewhere you know
start with melancholy & anger
spare no detail *& do* get sideways
to your heart   your spleen

Squeeze each drop from that dream
erase the contracts of the day
& in the long run-up to midnight
press forward   end run   end run

That area beyond the line of scrimmage
where defensive players widely scatter
broken field   broken field
smash down detail after detail

into one solid mess of a paragraph
        & call it a poem

Dreamland

Walls

It's like talking to the wall

The walls hear
but they are not listening

Walls form no opinions
a birth   a death   a wedding
it's all the same to walls

They wrap themselves
around your world
mask your nakedness
and keep you alone

A blank wall
dilutes your sorrow
defeats your joy
romances you
with that mark
where a picture once hung

But in the dark
in the best part of a dream
when the brain
            bathes itself with glymph
                    as pure as
                    spring water
the walls dream with you

August

to sleep in August
waves of heat shifting
to the beat of
the ceiling fan
is to risk a nightmare
doubly dreamt:
            a centipede
            crawls over
            wave of legs beating
            like the thousand
            whirring teeth
            of a 14th century
            torture device
            sawing
            into the spine
            of a peasant

the moon oscillates
on her path
sweat runs in rivulets
I shake awake:
            a tropical downpour
            runs through old
            stone gutters

Dream Scrubber

Ah, sweet night cometh & in the dark
you are the dream scrubber:
Neuronal Sorting in Progress.

Deep in your brain's hemispheres daylight moments
bleach clean & cerebellar folia-sorting switches ON
A day's worth of earthly hours pulse white to grey
crisscross.

Last night you wept in your beer
but tonight you're sorting sorrows into escrow.

Ran last in the 400 meter? Embed that data
into neural scars   pack it tight
reckon each moment its place
in the mix of remember and forget.

Lost high school sweetheart?
Sweep up the heart and put love away$_{1}$
lock the babe in the nucleus of sweethearts.

Engage Amygdala! Redo neurofibrils!
Sort, sort, sort the venal, hit and miss! hit and miss!
synapses flash & fire, misfire,
months years decades   *caution! caution!*
one thing leads to another (& dreamland
takes but a microsecond for its work).

At first light a mosquito embeds herself
in your forehead & *Shut down files!*

Ganglia untangle & with a yawn & a stretch,
you're ready for a new day of memories.

Not an Optimistic Sonnet

I have often dreamed
of a passageway
to something better
somewhere in a universe

where things don't wear out
but continue their perfect service
as I ride off, inspired, into a
brilliant sunset, every single thing

clicking in time behind me
clicking in perfect time
until that final dream (they take but
microseconds) where I am sitting

by an ancient fire listening for some
thing that slithers away in the night

The Crime

The psychological dimension, the little fractures and leaps and resolutions the poem enacts . . . the lean, muscular body of the sonnet free me ... to have aesthetic power while writing about the tragic situation of the individual in the world.

– Henri Cole

I dreamed I stood accused of a crime
I knew nothing of—a terrible act on a terrible
day and a terrible trial: in the dock
they railed against me. My love forsook me

the moment of the reading of my transgressions.
The jury was unswayed and I was ridden
to the gallows to await the death drop.
They were laughing at my plight

when all the King's horses were called in
to draw and quarter me in the town square
where they found my suchness so repulsive
that they freed me to live another day

and commit further crimes
of which I have no knowledge.

Dreams of Ice

At night my return from work
is marred by a metallic taste
something silvery & oxidized.
Why is it that smiles stand frozen
onto our faces at work
returned home, they twist into complaints?

I used to dream by day   taut thoughts
of wealth promotion raises   early retirement
now it's all dead space gone slack
formless, time barely edges it along.

Asleep's the only chance I get
but even those dreams are ravaged
by the insomniac night
except that one   that one
          about ice
where I am swimming deep in a lake
at the moment it turns to crystal
the shards of my day forming around me.

A Wallet of Real Leather

I dreamt I was living a watered-down
version of myself, a substitute me
who talked like me, only smarter.
In the dream I pulled my wallet

from my back pocket & it broke.
It came all apart. All apart.
Things were sticking out.
Handmade in Italy by Florentine

artisans, carried to me those
many miles by my lover
of many years, and now,
things were sticking out.

When I woke, sadly,
I checked my wallet.

Walls 2

There's a bright spot on the wall where a picture once hung,
an anti-shadow, its edges sharp on flowered wallpaper, it's
a black hole from far beyond the limit of Einstein's theories
& it sucks at the collapsing galaxies of my sorry little brain.

I match the spot on the wall to a portrait of the grandmother
I never knew, an old-country Slovak lost to the 1917 virus
who sleeps with no marker at her head, so solemn in
her homemade dress buttoned tight to the neck
her broach crusted over by a century under the lovely sod.

I hang my Grandma's portrait in its bright spot on the wall,
fits perfect, but it releases a Large Language Magellanic Cloud, the
Milky Way shivers, black holes start to sing
& scorpions spew forth, shouting:
"Surrender, Earthling! We have you outnumbered!"

The Music

Alphabet

A rising wind carries the scents of mastadons in rut & sloths
lumbering to their den to sleep. You look out at the sea, the land,
sweet sights of life, & you take up your smallest tool in darkness
—your talent still day-sharp— & shards, slivers, dust & facets fly.

You are telling your stories by firelight, your talent cutting
the stone you know so well into tiny ciphers of your invention.
So many dream of their language written in stone but you
honestly feel like you're starting to get your stories across:

the story of the hunt, of its blood & hide & bone & glory
the story of the sea and the land, their beauty, & the story
of how the sea & the land will be there for someone else
when these marks & lines & spaces, even this stone, are gone.

At daybreak you will take up your spear, its edges of chert
chipped sharp, & march with your fellows to the hunting ground.

The Music

At precisely midnight my Night Worry Syndrome strikes.
All day I dwelled on plate tectonics & now the bed posts shake
& I feel the continental crust shudder over earth's molten core
as I imagine the coast of Africa tucked into Manhattan &

visualize stone-age men drifting along the coastlines on a trickle
of human paths that coursed over earth's surface so late in our
planet's history. If you can't sleep, get up, though then, waking,
you'll suffer the moon's tidal push & gravity's pull ... still, I can't

help wondering what ancient weather gouged that lovely Moose River
thru solid granite? (And who am I to second guess plate tectonics?
Prof Heisenberg says we can't measure two things at one time.)
At peace with darkness, I'll return to my cooling sheets

to finish midnight's lost sleep, for a lifetime's but a blink of an eye
on this earth, and "you are the music, while the music lasts."[2]

Old Times

I dreamt there was a time when lightbulbs got hot,
when chivalry burned in our breasts young and old
and all the King's Men played poker till four a.m., then
went for the Farmer's Special of four eggs and ham.
A time when potatoes fried deep and fat ran in rivulets
through our veins. Craters did not yet pockmark the earth
nor did nuclear testing boil quartz into the shocked
polymorphic silicates coesite and stishovite
that today reflect, through their twisted latticework,
eyes grown weary of heavenly planetesimals
falling from the icy Kuiper belt: Our circles of fire
burn still, but hearts are leaden and once-chivalric
men quake at the dire-wolves that lurk
at light's edge, their wolfish jaws leering.

I, Iceman

While hiking I trip and fall
and am frozen into the glacier for 5000 years.
When found, I am taken to the medical examiner
who concludes after a complete post mortem
that I was a hunter gatherer
(fishing license in wallet)
from a coastal area
(tattoo of ship on chest)
who was killed en route to some sort of rite
(topless dancer ad in shirt pocket).

Further expert opinion suggests
we had a complex literature
(cocktail napkin with notes)
made primitive attempts
at extraterrestrial communication
(Walkman)
and appear to have been knowledgable
in drug therapies
(marijuana seeds in pocket).

Overall, they are amazed at how advanced we were
given the small size of our brains.

Pocketfuls of Time

The curve of Time is a burst star fragmented
and scattered, its small out-pouchings falling
in clusters, rolling into knots and tiny lumps
in the cosmic wind of an oscillating universe.

Digging into the pocket of your jeans amongst
the lint, your lucky stone, small change
you just might find one of these little boogers
whole, unworked, with all the raw
energy of its particular moment still in it.

From out your right pocket you pull a park bench.
It's in Zurich, where you're feeding pigeons & watching
old men shuffle by at closing time; sweepers
out of the middle ages pass with straw brooms.

That left pocket is more sinister.
It's got the times you've had a few too many
& the times you've had a few too many
friends die of cancer (jam those back).

And in your back pocket, your favorite,
you've just gotten your permit to drive
the fall leaves smell like cappuccino
the road twists beside the West Canada
Creek & in this, the sweetest pocketful of time

with your best pal as your navigator
you gas the TR3 around the curve.

Dry Bones

"We have invented nothing!"
– Pablo Picasso, after viewing Ice-Age
cave paintings in the south of France

It was three days of wind and rain and then
in one brilliant arc at the back of the house
between the pole and the meter (old wiring)
the electric went   and now
                                  it's back to the dark ages
                                  the stone age.

The days are quiet enough, but the nights: I find
you cannot save the daylight once dusk
creeps under it.   Outside
the Earth silently cools its crust &
vast fields of new vehicles stretch from city to city
without their harsh commercial light.
On the grid of our neighborhood
                                  foot to foot
people with wooden faces shift their weight.
                                    (I must step carefully
                                    in my hapless darkness.)

This thin candle holds a small world
its waxy yellow halo allows
that I may read before retiring
the collected works of some bullshit artist
who's mastered one genre, or another.

A steady drizzle falls in the long voice of the night
and at the very moment my dilated eyes close
                                        I see
we have invented nothing and nothing will remain
when the oceans roil into red dust, the only sound:
          dried bones clicking on cave bottoms
          dried bones clicking on cave bottoms
          dried bones clicking on cave bottoms

Cemetery Etiquette

Step around
its borders, virgin
sod slowly packing
this fresh grave you
searched for
under a hot morning sky
step around

Speak softly
though today she's
too deep
cooled and too deep for
those silly wind chimes
that, in the rising
noon breeze
speak softly

Don't mention certain
things, the gradual loss
of momentum, the shift
to out-of-focus: day before
yesterday she lay
in plain view, now she's
out of sight like some
secret life, like ashes
lightly packed, composting,
the heat gone out unnoticed
unmentioned

On Deaf Ears

Sunset at The Last Stop Inn and a man
tells the barmaid his girlfriend is dead
outside in the car, stabbed, and on the bar he sets
her severed finger, gold wrapped to catch the sunset

Up on a farm nearby an old man's talking about how
once she got the diabetes and started guarding her feet
it was over for them, separate rooms
" . . . and why's she have to talk about somethin' when
she doesn't know what in blazes she's talkin' about?"

On the bench in the garden you're saying
how funny it is that when the sun is setting here
it's rising somewhere else for other people to see
and I say, "Let's keep it to ourselves."

Now it's blue black sky, clear moon, candles inside
long dead and dripped away toward morning and your
words have dried up like those snails, once succulent
now cracked underfoot like some fragile, child's toy

"Let's keep it to ourselves"
What we thought we knew last night

Marion, Unmarried

she takes her job seriously now
needs the paycheck
lost that weight
blooms in new dresses
fingernails, grown out, are
shining in the white office light

perhaps she's between marriages
perhaps not, but
even the deepest black and blues
have yellowed & faded back
to the supple flesh of her teens

her kids don't bug her anymore

uncriticized, she works out
on her noon break
is taking up juggling in the evening
when, breathing freedom
        she happily opens herself
        to the silent night

My Friends

My friends the circus performers took the red eye
checked the tents the poles the elephants the tigers
crossed time zones from far flung continents ancient
and mysterious to visit our upstate farm for a long and deep

melatonin sleep. Emerged from their wagons, the elephants
pastured, they sat—a dime museum of human oddities—
around the kitchen wood stove, clutching hot coffee despite
the August heat. Tom Thumb sat with the dwarfs. Rubber man

stretched. *Remember the old Soviet Union?* asked the fat lady.
They loved us. And such a big country, said the trapeze artist.
I remember steam engines, said the tattooed man, removing
his shirt. Of course the 100-year-old man had the last word:

Remember the circus barges? When canals criss-crossed this
pretty country? It was a different time. It was a different time.

Lubricant

Quiet in our downtown lodging
We take our dulling fill
Of tea and smoldering
Marlboros, until

A siren blots the tick
Of Grandfather's clock
And a tank rolls near.
Only then we hear
What was always there—

The click click hum
As ball bearings whirr
In the sacrum
Of a monster.

Pools

Your first Christmas
tinsel shone double
in your crossed eyes.
With bits of lint
in your fists
you gurgled   cooed;
glowing bubbles rose from
your drool
like glass balls.

Now   you are slipping.

Like a still pool
in a forest cascade
curls under and spills
into the next
they slipped by you: twenty-nine
forty-nine   then sixty-nine
Christmas Days   each
cascading to a deeper
stiller pool beneath pines
without the glitter
of tinsel.

Moths

are eating
the fabric of our lives
unwoven   we are
burst & ragged holes
in the hollow garments
of Salvation Army
cloakrooms

air riders
eaters of tweed
floating without grace
on dusty grey wings
they show no finesse
for flight
but on their gleaming
shark teeth
saliva drips
like acid

our fabric weakened
woof torn from warp
we renew our search
for threads

Fragments

It was dark and the leaves had fallen
where you left me on the broad macadam
with your words ringing, the white eyes
of wolves, tiny moons along the roadside.

The news would report the explosion
& name the site where the hitchhiker's
heart blew up, scattering fragments
to throb in a dark Wisconsin field.

For years the roadside was littered with bits
of it quivering under a crust of snow, then ice
then thaw, then ice, then tonight, when specks
of light in a swollen firmament tally the years.

A miracle of age, this heart, its red core
                    elastic and whole again.

In The Garden First Thing

Caught in the cyclonic suck of a monumental headache
I ride the steep wind of the universe's pain (with you,
some mornings are like this: hungover, no breeze).
Dare I estimate the weight of the universe today?

Or how fast its expansion? It seems collapse is already
underway as we watch the herbs drip & the snails
fist it out with the slugs. A pockmarked moon dims
overhead; somewhere cold black stars implode,

but here on the garden bench my cerebellum is hotter
than the flick of the Bic at the tip of your second smoke
of the day. Look! By your foot! A roach encroaches! Worms
twist, defecating, just inches below this frail crust of earth,

that bit of mint, these fingers of oregano invading
the thyme. Up from the garden bench (stretch, more coffee)
the evanescent scents of tarragon, basil & sage
defy the dark matter that congeals at our edges.

I feel the pull of strong gravity.
                    In its grasp I am a weak force.

Return of the Tree Frog

In the spring I tire of dark career moves
& the long hard daylight forces
a transformation in the teeth of my failures:
        I find my voice
        & it is the voice of a frog.

But not those metamorphosed pollywogs!
that roil up countless out of mad mud
to spend their lives on the silent bottom
where eyeless salamanders hunt by touch.
Mine is the voice of the ethereal tree frog
        enthroned overhead on thin leaves
this frog never drinks; rather he absorbs water
through his delicate undersurface
& when swollen
to the desired state of hydration
        he feasts solely on the larva
        of the sphinx moth.

Each morning he tumbles, unharmed,
down tropical layers of vegetation
to rest in the hot afternoon in low beds
of wild oregano; then, at sunset
he climbs over multicolored fruits
& slips past parrots and toucans
to again gain those rare leaves
        where he will feed and chirp
        in the essential perfume of evening.

Haiku

tree frog perched
on strand of lemon grass
delicate chirping

The Lichen

This partially stolen sonnet lauds "the delightful
web of partnership and contingency"[3] that is the lichen,
fungi and algae paired in perfectly symbiotic couples,
the fungus providing the body, or thallus, while the alga

fixes dinner in a linked relationship that's life-long (though
Jimmy Carter's marriage was longer). If only my last
marriage had had such nourishing rhythm! and not
the unkempt cadence broken and ragged those years we

shared a kitchen packed with so many unused machines that
a humble lichen (being neither animal nor mineral) would wonder
Why? Why must they take out from the corner bodega?
The walls of my lonely heart shudder at our bodega owner's

cruel refusal to let my love hold a place in line for me, so that
I abandoned *our* symbiosis to go hungry in my present solitude.

Sunrise/Sunset

After sunset
we are the lovers of the century.
Tasting costly truffles
in each other's mouth
I am Valentino, you – Garbo
and the corks are popping
until, too soon, the sunrise comes

Chocolate hangover: this morning
I am brushing love from my teeth

In the Eighth Round

It might have been better
if she hadn't been so sexy, the big tease
from the moment the long hot morning sky
faced us that endless day   then, lounging
on her afternoon break   holding up her hands
that way she does

In the Swiss Alps there is no dusk
just the sudden drop of evening
(and sexy in daylight gets sexier in the dark)
It might have been better had we just talked
and not each all over the other, in the clinch
the grace going from her face
as we fought
for the title   both
on the canvas   down
for the count   in the eighth round

Fifty Years Together

The years going blank behind them
an old couple loses the last thread
of dusk in the blue black night.

Fifty years in a cocktail haze,
together they stand by the gas heater
energy dissipating, mucosal surfaces drying
the old battlefields of their island kingdom
long healed. (Though the entrance
wound of her love is still fresh in his chest):

    "Make me a cup of coffee, would you, Hon?"
    "You know damn well I don't drink coffee."
    ". . . but ... you're still my cup of tea."

Sleepless mammals in a sterile silence
there's the slick glint of 30's cocktail glasses
    & overhead, the young, sullen moon's
    a glowing afterthought.

Texas Red Pine

standing here on texas red pine finished glossy
for a century some fundamental structure shakes
buckles rocks like a ship in a gale open sea
open sea and here we are you and me as alone
as two people can be with one headache split
between them while the night worn thin becomes
a sweaty morning with its arc of blood shot sun
like a streak of lead poisoning the sky
Christ it's hot, you say and of course as always
you are right you are right and I have a lot
to learn ... perhaps from you with your last word
your black ultimatum, *can't go on like this*
          perhaps from some other

Marriage #2

you broke up my marriage
but when I was
        happily unmarried
                you blew
                an occasional breeze
                through porch screens

I tried for #2
        happily married
                I was becalmed
                (except for a rare, warm gust)

tonight
        unhappily married again
                the doors are blowing shut
                then, blown open
                        they reveal you
                        across every room

The Photography of Birds

Those who photograph birds
go by twos to their blinds because
they know that birds cannot count.

When a pair enters their blind
the birds are silent
until one birdwatcher leaves
and, thinking the blind empty, the birds
will sing to their young as they
regurgitate a pulp of shrimp
or patch some sagging drywall
with a stucco
of fishing line and feather.

We are the counters.   We know
how many birds are sliced to bits
by cell phone towers each year.

We decide what to count
but still cannot tell why
that grackle veered   crazed
into the upstairs windowpane
this afternoon   or how
one comes to such a suicide.

Every night of your life
you sleep in some bed
counting sunsets
and after the night's rainfall
your soles resonate with death
as you squash a dozen or more
lives on your backyard path.

Can you think these bursting snails
this murmur of souls   won't count?

Snapshots

In strip after strip
of old negatives
celluloid women
surround me
    vignetted by time
    we are all
    the photographer's props.

Who are these soft-focus ladies?
A lifetime never spent
lies just beyond sharp focus:
    a kingdom never come
    some other will
    than mine be done.

The strips hold
a coarsely granular
yet intimate image
    (a kiss   arms
              over shoulders)
but what is seen
is only a snapping
shutter's breath
of what was missed.

Blow Bubble Blow

On the evening of first hearing
of your first wife's deteriorating
mental condition you are blowing
bubbles in an empty parking lot.

You found a child's bubble outfit
on the macadam, so you're launching shape
shifters of sunlight bending & bursting
among the pines & into the setting sun.

Your lips purse, cheeks puff, alveoli expand,
you are dizzy with oxygen & the commotion
of bubbles in motion in the cool summer
air.   Weak with guilt, you watch

            frail skins of soap
            wobble into the night.

Saloon Keeper's Son

These Hands

I've seen these hands before,
these hands about to cut oregano
in the morning shade where the garden's
rose-colored brick border molders,
snails walk their slimy trails
& a toad sits round as a pudding
awaiting the promise of rain.
I've seen these hands before.

I saw them first as a child in the Bronx
in grandfather's barbershop, hands
with knuckles widened by 40 years
of straight razors stropped & scissors wielded
20's and 30's mustaches trimmed pencil-thin.
As a teenager I saw them again
crossed in grandpa's casket.
(Why do they fold them like that? To show peace
& repose I suppose, but it's a hard & cold repose.)

Years later I saw the hands again, hands without
malice, without violence, the hands of my father
a machinist's hands hung thick-veined over lathe
or drill press, where razor-thin metal curlicues sparkle
on the shop floor & later I saw them laid on the beloved
mahogany bar top of his very own saloon, hands
proudly sliding a manhattan toward a customer.
(They folded those hands, too soon too soon.)

The morning light turns grey with weather
& in the near distance thunder rolls over the bay.
Eyes down, I rush to cut oregano for my sauce.

Going into Caves

there's that chapter to write and fish to fry
the coils of the fridge are keening with dust
& backslider you backslider you're dreaming of caves
in an upstate summer when a boy of eleven discovers

a crevice no one in the club ever knew was there
coolness from it the smell of a small dead mammal
the boy slips in tight scrawny enough against limestone
slick with glacier water that's sought the sea for eons

his trusty scout light's two D batteries beat the blackness
back an enormous room its candle wax walls luminous
stunning stone pagodas the slow drip of stalactites
the pound of his heart the fear of flash flooding

then a glint of sunlight a prelude to sorrow on fields
of alfalfa drying beyond the narrow passage out

Uncle Steve

For Mother"s Day
I am printing an old negative
of Steve:
        my mother's brother
        who was never my uncle
        because of a war
        before my birth.

His picture comes up gently
in the developer:
Steve the athletic brother
        a gymnast, elected most popular
        shot down in '43
                to flop
                with the other uncles
                in the sands of Anzio.

Silent grains of silver blacken.

My mother, seeing
his high school grin
will remember like yesterday
when the news came back:
        a whole platoon
        dead on the hot white sand
        others bobbing in the surf
        while the hard Italian sun
        baked the stucco
        of a captured village.

Mother will prefer to fix his image
at an earlier time:
        standing on his hands
        on the beach at Lavalette
        his mouth the kindest
        of all the kids
        talking of enlisting.

For Mother's Day
        silvery whiteness gives way
        to a B&W smile.

Thursday Is Garbage Day

Already in my slippers after work, with dripping bag in hand I shuttled surreptitiously from the old house down the alley to the dumpster, the one that belongs to the apartment complex on the corner, and there was my father sitting inside the dumpster in his best summer suit, the light grey one with the wide lapels, wide tie, too. Pencil thin Errol Flynn mustache. He was holding a bowl of American cherries. "Hey, Dad," I said. He popped a cherry into his mouth. "They were wrong," he said, chewing. "I'm not dead." He caught the look on my face. "Honest, son. . ." "Right," I said, "and for thirty years nobody said anything? I was there, Dad. The tubing, the wires pulsing and then quiet, and afterward, all those cakes on the table, the kielbasas." He closed his watery-blue eyes and nodded. When he opened them again his eyes looked like pennies, old, dark ones. He spit out a pit. "How about an espresso?" he said. The black of the coffee, the ritual stirring in of sugar. "You need to do better, son," he said. "Buckle down." Well into my 50s, I shuttled back to the house, and dark fell quickly that night before the garbage pickup, I remember.

Half Full

Half full of moon
and stale with age
I grope at a lukewarm snack
while the wobbly ceiling fan
beats dust around
my sad little kitchen.

Numbed by the novocaine
of a class reunion
I will sit with my snack
on the moonlit
upstairs porch
to dwell on past moons
    and the bright eyed youths
    who saw them.

The Wheel Horse

The slip and the slide
of being in the work week
brings its risks. One moment
you're tops, you're bent to the task

the wheel horse
the next moment
you're thinking maybe
you will or maybe you won't.

The week's shot anyway;
at day's end we hardly
seem responsible
for the way things went, when

out of the dark come the sounds
of rain, thunder, and wind.

Things to Do This Weekend

cut the baby's nails   cut your own nails
duct tape the cracked garbage can

shovel dog turds out of backyard
buy Liquid Plumber
give the dog a bath
          give yourself a bath
watch the kids play 'chop the dog'

spray for roaches
duct tape around the air conditioner
bitch to the neighbor
                    about
                         his barking
                              dog

duct tape that rusted-out headlight
call the state adolescent unit
                    to see how your oldest son is

feed the dog   feed the kids
                         buy more chips

break up a fight over who's Peter Pan
take out the garbage   drop off the recycle
give the kids their antibiotics
                    take your antibiotic

swat flies
find the pacifier
find a bigger can for under the leaking
               dishwasher

teach the kids to pitch a softball
duct tape the dining room window

mop up milk   put flea stuff on the dog
duct tape the broken trike seat
duct tape the broken toy sword
tell the neighbor his kid
          needs to be on Ritalin

check the football pool!
check your lottery ticket!
buy more duct tape

Curriculum Vitae

I woke to the sound of rain on tin thrumming
drumming the roof of which I am so proud,
but today I must update my curriculum vitae
so I spend the morning admiring the moss

greening on the north-facing bark of the maples;
the entire afternoon I watch the corn grow.
Why is there no place to list one's disappointments?
This small life! This small life! Look up to blue heaven;

there, at the outer reaches of the Oort Cloud,
a shell of cometary bodies spins beyond
the orbit of Pluto. Space: such a perfect word
for the nothingness, the rare clods of frozen

ammonia, ice, the space dust and detritus
                    from which we men were made.

Waiting for Postage

an emphysematous poet
is standing in line
at the post office
        his packages tug
        at dusky integument
        stretched thin
        over hollow bone

this art deco building
once echoed with the heel taps
of young flappers clicking along
in the stainless steel glitter
        now   moldy and grey
                it resonates with a truncate
                bronchitic cough
                from deep in a barrel chest

through the out-of-town slot
expectant editors recline
in their urban interstices
the poet waits bowed over
his mouth a puffing 'O'
he doesn't know anyone in line
and the click of the postage scale
reminds him of the green tanks
                of his oxygen addiction

the long wait
& stamps thin as a gasp
sliding over slick worn marble
        the lovely civil servant
        makes small change

testing his tongue
he licks the glaze from blue lips
tries to catch his breath
thinks of his dry writing
        being read
                objectively

Blood Songs

Blood Song

I keep asking but no one seems to know:
Why do they keep coming to get their hearts?

Down here in the Surgical Pathology Laboratory
          we don't see patients often.
The pale green walls quiver with anticipation
when one is coming   like the stunned walls
of their heart came quivering in a stainless pan
          the day of their transplant.
We simply don't know what to say.
Would they like it in a jar? a brown paper bag?
wet or dry? formalin? alcohol?

Years ago they came for their gallstones
to set them out, split and multifaceted
(strictly ornamental)
but a heart?   failed & flabby
without its thump   its gallop
on the coffee table?

One woman, just out of Recovery
her anorexia hanging loosely
wanted only to hold her old heart.
My diary wouldn't be complete without a look
she said & under the fluorescent light she turned it
pale and forlorn like fatigued metal
its concrete arteries   dark worms on its surface.
She spoke of how so very long ago
it had pounded out its rhythm
in the springtimes of her youth.

Some come to bury them
but most – like her – come to look
pay their respects   then
turning toward the door
they leave with another heart
the long-awaited harvest
singing its new blood song.

Insert Card Below

This morning
insert four days of illness
into your life:
        a double room full of
        high fever, nausea
        extreme shortness of breath.

During insertion
there will be a pause.
Like a plastic card
being counted
deep in its slot
all further events are postponed
the future is suddenly tentative.
        (The end of this
        phase of illness
        will be marked
        by a depressing
        metallic taste.)

Your card's worth
is recorded
on an unseen magnetic strip:
        it may be used again at any time
        but one day
        it will have no residual value.

The Moon

was a faint smile riding out
on an east wind when
you called with the bad news
about the biopsy

now I understand, you said
a positive biopsy
is not a positive thing

after your call a sudden flow
of southern stars
startled me & I looked up
as one held underwater
will glance at the surface
while he struggles
in his medium.

Sundowners

> *Sundowning: a sudden deterioration of mental status in those with Alzheimer's disease, typically occurring late in the day.*

blueblack
night drops quickly
stunned darkness to
greater darkness flows
across the grain of dusk

the sundowners
now in steep slippage
roam wild hills
mount boundaries that, to them
seem bright as day

insomniac
they are strewn out against time
skin and soft tissues give way
their arms grope at steep walls
for some vague moment of clarity

his mind, a stranger,
yields to the Irish hills
the burdock
while she fights a rising damp
simple tasks
forgotten
brick by brick dismantled
as if some ablated organ
has left her emptier now
so that he just
rubs her the wrong way
at the distant
forgotten edges
of day

Today, You Are Lecturing

up front, getting to them
before they're in the clinics treating patients

today they show interest but it is a passing interest
in a case you can't forget: the anatomy of domestic violence
the mode, the manner of death, a fatal wound opened
with the stainless flash of a thrift shop steak knife
tight between her ribs, a thin wound spitting red
while the refrigerator growls in the background

they always ask and you always tell them
Don't pull out the knife! but young minds wander
and you, buffoonish professor walking across campus
with your fly open, you tell them stop! stop it now!
about the dollar signs, what's "reimbursable"
we're all of us living under penalty of death
there are no commuted sentences

think! you are saying, think it out!
in the same moment that you are thinking of how
you will trace their lives into the future

and how the future isn't what it used to be[4]

Einstein Took The Train

In his last days Albert Einstein traveled
by rail to Houston where a repair of his
abdominal aortic aneurysm (an experimental
procedure at the time) was considered.

Einstein took the train.
Halfway from New Jersey
he threw the coach's window
open to the summer night.

In Houston, DeBakey waited
insomniac, he paced his O.R.
checking & re-checking
fitting & fashioning the Dacron
graft for the dilated aorta that lay
like a fat postprandial python
in Albert's warm belly.

Einstein studied the sudden planets
sprawling in an uneasy firmament.
He searched the odd and angulated
corners of his mind, watching time
curve off into the tepid night sky
he was shocked & terrified by the swirls
of cosmic dust that sprang up around him
as they will around men of shaken faith.

Weakened, he rolled slow past glassy bayous
and with each clack clack clack of steel wheel
on rail   with each systolic thump
the walls of the python shuddered.

When he saw the Houston skyline rise
jagged on the grassy plain the sleepless genius
sighed at it   & at the phosphenes
that began to dance across his eyelids
like a blood-red Milky Way come leaking
leaking   a dam
about to burst
with the look of the sky at night.

Crossing State Lines

Farr, Texas

In Farr
when they're not talking
about football scores
    they talk
    about each other

From Farr
it's a long bus ride
to anywhere
but Texas Bus Lines
will take you there
(though there's
    no smoking in the coach
& there are desperados
along the route)

Bus station slime
rings the Farr urinal
    & the Men's Room walls
    glow with perversity

Rarely
someone returns to Farr
& buying the ticket
is always the same:
    Where you goin'?
        —To Farr, Texas
    Goin' to Farr, eh?
        —Yeah. It's where I'm from

COCKTAIL

mix myself up a little cocktail and sip it slow before dinner while the can of soup is cooking all brown and steamy in the kitchen and that of course is where I am sipping the cocktail while the gulf breeze is simmering hot and the cocktail glass is dripping wet & ice cube cold and I mean colder than the mornings when I went up to the Saint Lawrence River fishing without you dear in the late summer of the year we parted maybe it was August and in the evening after fishing all day while I fried perch on the shore missing you & the wind shifted into the north coming real cold straight across the river from Canada the sky clear night crashing down around me millions of stars punctate overhead and the northern lights rippling like a curtain a really high one   & now I am simply sipping this cocktail

Tree Frogs

Where the path
gently curved in ferns
and damp forest floor
the furniture company
is taking out logs;
    this stand of old maple
    now an ugly swath
    where the curved path
    had been. Not a scar yet
    but a fresh wound widening
        (and I see where they
        are marking the maples
        on my other path
        with bright orange
        slashes).

The frogs
have abandoned their bogs:
    frogs are the first to go
    especially the peepers;
    later the hardier species
    with thicker integument
    will follow.

This June evening
I continue
to scratch out words
as if the frogs
still chirped
in the trees.

The Still Woods

Hot from skiing
over slow granular
I stop
to eat some snow.

The best is picked
off a pine tree:
        sharp sap &
        mint
        from a time when
        the arctic north
        belonged to silence.

As I chew icy & wet
spiced needles
        the acid odor
        of gasoline engines
        fills the still woods.

Full of Fall

The woods are full of fall
It lies thick on the trail
lends its scent to the thin October fog
like a sharp fermented cheese or last
night's beer gone sour

Out early on this grey morning
with wretched tendons rattling in their sheaths
I am hiking in a steady acid drizzle
over streams the color of tea
I've come to see the leaves, the birds
before the first snow hits
but my loons   my Canada geese
are gone from the northern bog
already they course along ancient
flyways on imaginary magnetic lines
        They've left me on this glacial moraine
                alone

I try to think of hopeful things
like filling next year's calendar
but hiking back in the dusky woods
I feel only a cold moon
the whisper of the north wind
and then (am I dreaming?)
beyond that stand of balsam
I hear the scratch of an oyster catcher's
pencil thin beak in tepid island sand
a roseate spoonbill adrift on brackish water?
are there Hudsonian godwits flitting
among black terns?

        & overhead
        the laughing gulls are laughing

Geese

While picking pecans
I saw them overhead:
          Canada geese
          in the fall
                    fog.

Ragged V-shape
in cool low clouds
they spell each other
as runners in a long race
will tuck in behind
          other runners
          to break the
                    wind.

An oracle from the North
A windswept foil forecasting
a warm January
with lazy, truncate days &
short-sleeved bicycling;
but these northern birds
gone south could
not foresee
          the cold cold spring
          that froze the salty
          foam balls on the beach
          & anchored the foolish loons
          in the grey mud flats.

Loon

daft bird
soaring he crashes
onto the still lake
dives to 100 feet
        and stays

red eye for depth vision
red eye for madness
with bones dense as stone
        for ballast
he swims along the clear blue bottom
mouth opened wide   then returns
to the nest
to regurgitate
        rock bass
        for his young

yodeling his maleness
he dances in shallow reed beds
with stealth in his manic eye
where, curved along the retina,
Gods of Thunder
watch decaying piney shores
collapse
        into the laughing lakes
        of the Algonquin

The Ice

The holidays are come and done
two weeks well passed, the solstice gone
gale winds grown faint &
we are discarding congealed gravy

With the last run to the airport
the relatives vanish north
speaking of Alzheimer's
divorces   Uncle Johnny's lung mass;
a wintry mix awaits them
icy roads, a sheet of glass

Now   here
timed to the movement of your heart
you pace along the tepid sand
the moon is up
the tide swells and, receding
brings memories of the ice

Somewhere lake-effect snow
lies thick on the picnic tables
of an empty campsite
where the stream is frozen to stone

Northern lights flicker then dim
in the stillness
a wintry moon is etched in ice
You cannot forget quickly
despite the sweet warm moon
the tide
you cannot forget quickly
the ice

The Thaw

last of december
a new calendar's hung
and christmas tree needles
drop into compost   last week
the woods were under the worst of
                        winter
and came an early thaw   fog billowed
off the dirty snow   rain drummed
on logs with frozen rot revealed

I am hiking in vegetation deceived
by that warm south wind
wood laurel   moss   fern
trilliums and lady slippers
ground pine and partridge berry
tricked into greening out of time
but then the wind creaks into the north
the spruce   blue against blue
rise like tall ships in the shifting
                    wind
and I am before the mast
the pine cone rigging groans
the temperature   drops

I try to memorize this place
where ice shatters like fine crystal
before I must chart a course
through the cold   congealing
        Adirondack bog

Endnotes

1. Emily Dickinson: “The Bustle in a House”
2. T.S. Eliot, Four Quartets
3. Adirondack Explorer, June 2024
4. Statement attributed to Yogi Berra.

www.ingramcontent.com/pod-product-compliance
Lightning Source LLC
LaVergne TN
LVHW051015080826
845145LV00009B/2633